My First Montessori Book of Numbers

MARY DA PRATO

First Published 2013
This revised edition, 2014

ISBN: 1484147537
ISBN-13: 978-1484147535

DISCLAIMERS

In this publication, students are referred to as "he" while guides are called "she." This designation, assigned for the reader's convenience, in no way reflects the gender dynamic in a Montessori classroom.

Diagrams in the "For Parents" section of *My First Montessori Book of Numbers* are not drawn to scale due to computer program limitations and page size restrictions.

"Cards and Counters" is an activity designed for children ages four and older who already have experience with accurate counting and a strong Montessori foundation. While "zero" is not explored with Cards and Counters, the symbol "0" appears in this book beside a blank page. The concept of zero is officially introduced during an exercise known as "Spindle Boxes." Cards and Counters and Spindle Boxes are described in detail in the "For Parents" section of this publication.

Always supervise your child when working with small objects. Store all cards and counters in a safe place away from children under four years of age as counters can be a choking hazard.

HOW TO USE THIS BOOK

My First Montessori Book of Numbers is designed for children who have a solid understanding of the quantities and numbers one through ten as presented in the Primary Montessori Casa, or classroom for three through six year olds. Before viewing the contents of this book with your child, make sure he has mastered all preliminary skills related to quantity and symbol recognition from one to ten inclusively. Keep in mind that many young children who can allegedly count to ten are simply repeating a memorized sequence without understanding what numbers actually represent. For preliminary mathematics exercises, please refer to *My First Montessori Book of Quantities* by Mary Da Prato.

In this book, "0" is represented by a blank page. Point to the symbol "0" and say, "zero." Then point to the blank page and say, "Zero means there is nothing here." When counting the red dots in this book, point to the numeral and say its name. Then point to the red dot on the facing page and count, "one." When counting more than one red dot, point to the top left dot first as you count, "one." Then point to the top right dot and say, "two." Count the next row of dots from left to right as in the previous row. Continue saying, pointing, and counting throughout the text, counting systematically from left to right, top to bottom. Counting systematically from left to right starting at the top of the page reinforces the manner in which children in the Casa lay out red wooden disks during an activity called "Cards and Counters," the inspiration for this book.

O

1

2

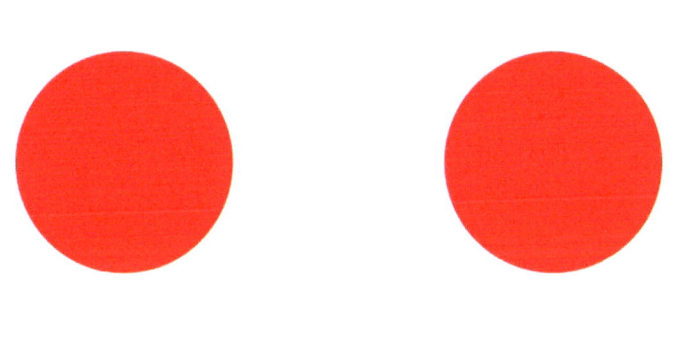

3

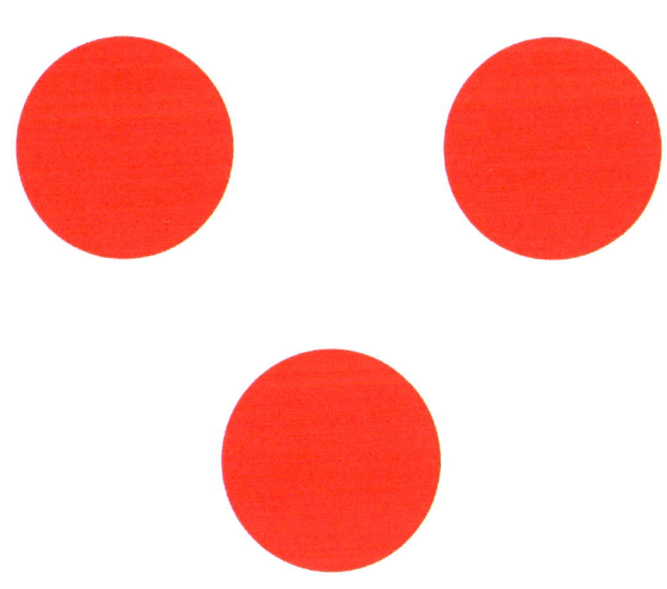

4

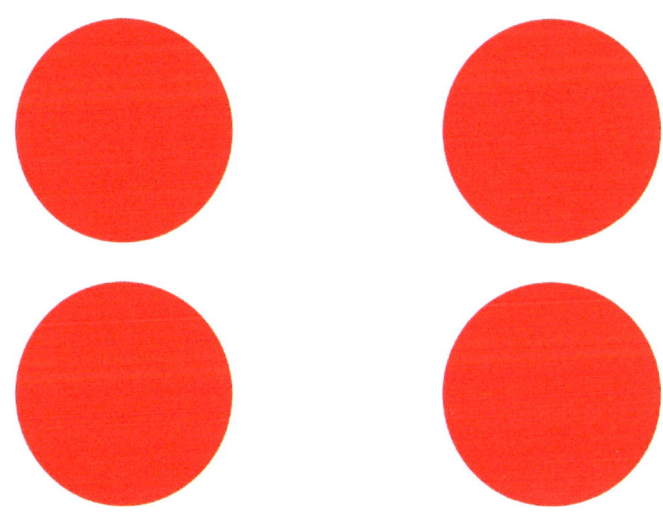

5

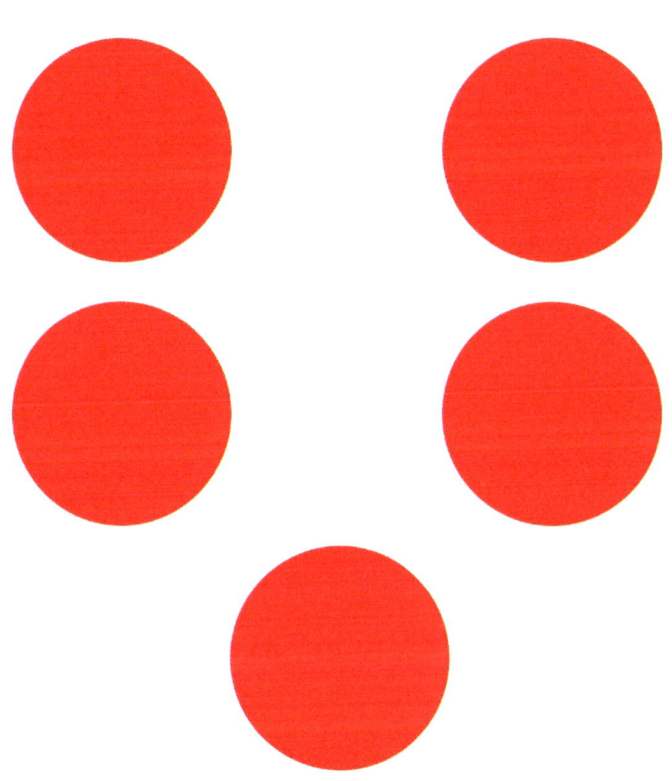

6

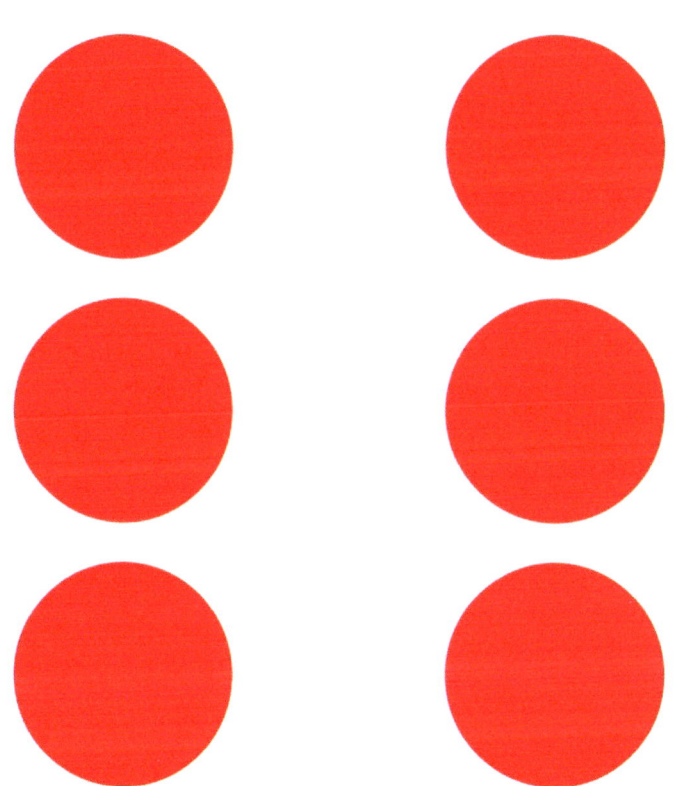

7

8

9

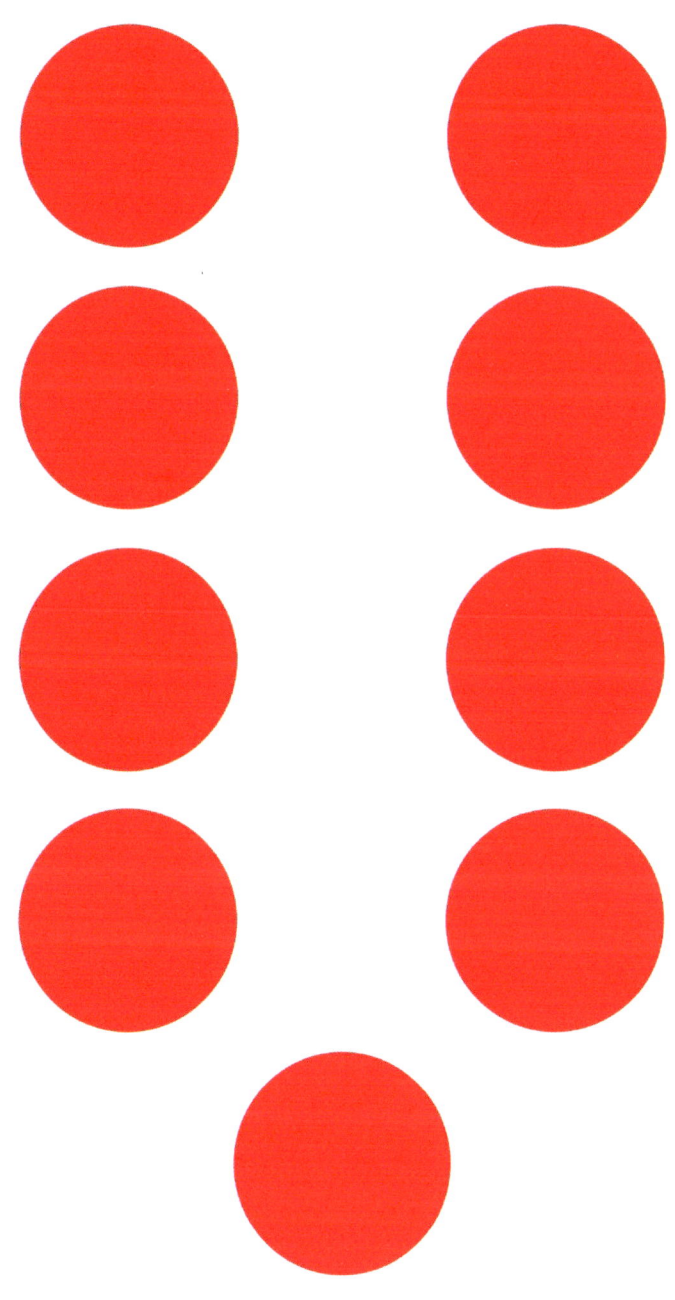

10

FOR PARENTS

My First Montessori Book of Numbers uses symbols inspired by the hands-on math exercise "Cards and Counters." This activity is introduced to children approximately four years of age in the Primary Montessori prepared environment following mastery of all prerequisite skills described in *My First Montessori Book of Quantities*.

Number Rods

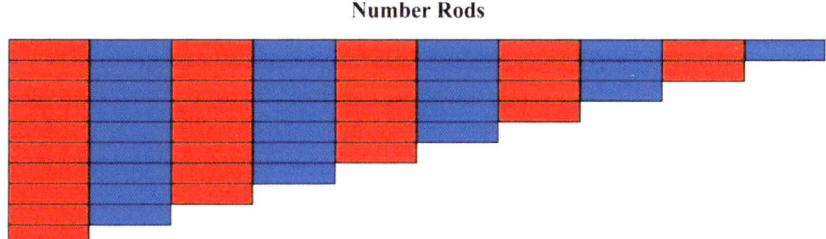

Before a student in the Montessori Casa receives his first presentation with Cards and Counters, several preliminary skills must be mastered. The first mathematics lesson presented is "Number Rods," equally segmented attached bars that concretely illustrate quantities from one through ten. Each segmented Number Rod represents quantity as an isolated entity, a vital prerequisite for eventually counting sets of objects. Counting each segment of every Number Rod with the whole palm of the hand from left to right helps instill the following concepts:

- Each quantity is a single entity that exists in isolation from other quantities.
- Each quantity has a name.
- Each number can be represented by a single object rather than by a collection of loose objects. "Five," for example, is represented by a single Number Rod divided into five attached segments of equal size and alternating colors instead of five individual objects such as five separate buttons.

- Quantities can be represented with physical objects or with numerical notation.
- Numbers follow a specific sequence.
- Using segmented bars for counting rather than loose objects clarifies the definition of quantity as an isolated entity. Introducing loose objects for counting before this foundation has been laid often confuses the child and delays mathematical comprehension.[1]
- Work with the Number Rods and their accompanying Number Cards indirectly prepares students for addition, subtraction, multiplication, and division.

Learning to count from one through ten with the Number Rods is reinforced through a number of distance memory games in which the child must retrieve a requested Number Rod from a second location in the classroom. A solid understanding of quantities one through ten indicates readiness to learn numerical symbols which are introduced through "Sandpaper Numerals."

---

[1] Montessori, Maria. *Dr. Montessori's Own Handbook*. Mineola: Dover Publications, 2005. Print. Pages 119-124.

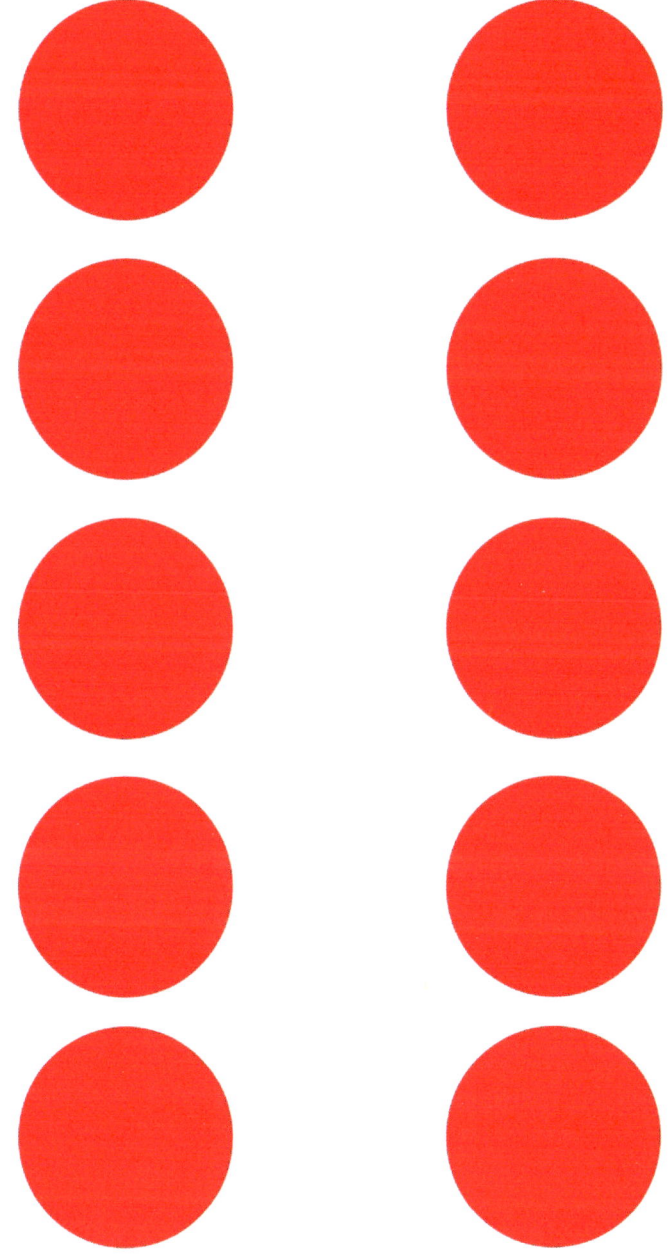

Sandpaper Numerals

Once a student understands how to count quantities from one through ten, numerical symbols 0-9 are introduced through individual Sandpaper Numerals mounted on separate pieces of painted green wood. By tracing each Sandpaper Numeral with the dominant index and middle fingers, a child acquires a motor memory of numerical symbols. Sandpaper Numerals introduce and reinforce the following concepts:

- Symbols for the quantities 0-9 are introduced and practiced.
- Sandpaper Numerals unlock the door to the world of written numbers.
- Tracing Sandpaper Numerals in correct stroke sequence with the index and middle fingers prepares the hand and mind for writing numerals.
- Memorization of numerical symbols introduced through the Sandpaper Numerals is an essential prerequisite to the presentation "Number Rods and Cards" in which students learn to associate quantities and symbols for one through ten.

Mastery of Sandpaper Numerals 1-9 ("0" can be introduced later through the Spindle Boxes) indicates readiness for Number Rods and Cards, a series of exercises in which a student learns to label Number Rods with their corresponding numerical symbols. Matching Number Rods to their corresponding numerical cards illustrates quantity as an entity, the association between quantity and its numerical representation, and the sequence of numerical symbols. Additionally, Number Rods indirectly prepares students for addition, subtraction, multiplication, and division.

Number Rods and Cards at Random

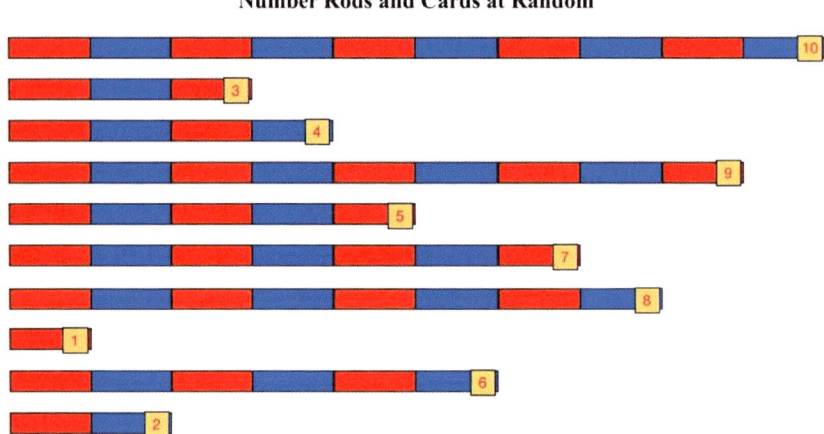

Number Rods, Sandpaper Numerals, and Number Rods and Cards presentations are described in detail in *My First Montessori Book of Quantities*.

Spindle Boxes in Progress

Accuracy and confidence with all Number Rods and Cards activities indicate readiness for "Spindle Boxes," a set of manipulatives which allow a child to organize quantities into sets. Spindle Boxes introduce and reinforce the following concepts:

- Spindle Boxes highlight sets of quantities.
- Numerical symbols represent a specific quantity of separate objects.
- The concept of zero as an empty set is introduced.
- Zero's numerical symbol, "0," is officially taught.
- The natural, recursive sequence of numerals 0 through 9 is reinforced.
- 0-9 are the only numerical symbols in our number system. Spindle Boxes lay a foundation for the understanding that any real number, regardless of the size of the quantity, is written using only the numerical symbols 0-9.

In the Montessori Casa for three through six year olds, a child who has mastered all Number Rods and Cards activities receives the presentation "Spindle Boxes." The Spindle Boxes consist of numbered compartmentalized boxes, an additional box or basket for storage, forty-five loose spindles or wooden dowels for counting, and eight fasteners to tie sets of spindles together. Fasteners for grouping spindles can be made of Velcro® strips, a bead on a cord, elastic with a snap, a strip of cloth with a button, or lengths of ribbon, yarn, or string. Fasteners vary in length to accommodate different sizes of spindle sets. The fastener for "2" is the shortest while the fastener for "9" is the longest. Since "1" does not constitute a set of quantities, no fastener is used when counting "one." When not in use, fasteners and loose spindles are placed in the storage container.

To begin the Spindle Boxes presentation, the guide and child gather all components of the Spindle Boxes and bring them to a table. Once the materials are laid out on the table as illustrated in "Spindle Boxes in Progress," the guide quickly assesses the child's ability to recognize numerical symbols by having him count the numbers printed on the Spindle Boxes aloud from "1" to "9." It is not necessary for the child to know how to read "0" yet, but he is welcome to count aloud from "0" to "9" if he knows how. If the child cannot count accurately or hesitates during the assessment, the guide asks him to count a few more times and gives assistance as needed. The Spindle Boxes and their accompanying materials are then put away for a later time. The student's inability to count accurately and confidently indicates that he needs additional practice with the preceding lesson, Number Rods and Cards. For more information about Number Rods and Cards, consult *My First Montessori Book of Quantities.*

If the student can accurately identify each symbol printed on the Spindle Boxes from "1" to "9," the guide officially begins her presentation. She starts by removing one spindle from the storage container with her dominant hand. The guide then passes the spindle she is holding to the palm of her non-dominant hand as she counts aloud, "one." After she has counted "one," the guide closes her non-dominant hand around the single spindle and feels its weight and size. As she places the single spindle into the Spindle Box compartment labeled with the number "1," the guide says, "one." A fastener is not wrapped around the single spindle as it does not constitute a set of quantities.

"Two" is the first quantity that uses a fastener or binder. Before counting "two," the guide opens or unties the shortest fastener and places it in the bottom of the compartment labeled "2." Laying the open fastener across the bottom of the Spindle Box compartment before continuing makes it easier to tie spindles together after they are counted. After preparing the fastener, the guide takes a spindle out of the storage container with her dominant hand and transfers it to her non-dominant hand as she counts aloud, "one." To make "two," the guide removes a second spindle from the storage container with her dominant hand and passes it to her non-dominant hand. As the guide passes the second spindle to her non-dominant hand, she counts "two." There are now two spindles in her non-dominant hand. She closes her hand around the two spindles to feel their size and weight. The guide says "two" as she simultaneously places the two spindles into the Spindle Box compartment labeled "2" so they rest on top of the fastener. Once the two spindles are in their correct compartment, the guide ties them together with the fastener to indicate they are a set. The guide lays out the fastener in the "3" compartment and demonstrates counting three spindles in the same manner used to count two spindles. After finishing her demonstration, the guide transfers the activity to the child. Under the guide's supervision, the student finishes counting out spindles for compartments "4" through "9." The child should use the same counting technique as the guide in order to receive a clear sensorial impression of larger sets of quantities becoming bigger and heavier. As the bundles increase in size, it may be necessary for the child to use two hands to transfer the spindles to their correct compartment. This is perfectly acceptable as long as the child's method of counting allows him to feel the increased size and weight of the sets of spindles.

When the child is finished counting, the guide points out how there are no more spindles left in the storage container. Even though no spindles remain, there is still one more compartment in the Spindle Boxes, the zero compartment. The guide points to the symbol "0" printed on the Spindle Boxes and says, "This is called 'zero.' It means 'nothing.'" Once the child understands the meaning of zero, the guide demonstrates how to return the spindles to the storage container starting with the "9" compartment. The guide unfastens the binder around the bundle of nine spindles and removes the nine spindles from the compartment simultaneously. By removing the spindles altogether, the baric and tactile perceptions of spindle sets are retained. She places these spindles into the storage box simultaneously without counting. The guide then removes the opened fastener from the bottom of the "9" compartment and lays it out flat in the storage container. Spindles from compartment "8" are then put away in the same manner. Fasteners are stacked from long to short in the storage container for ease of use.

Once all spindles and fasteners have been returned to the storage container, the guide transfers the activity to the student by saying, "Now it's your turn. You can work with this as much as you want." A Montessori guide is careful to choose words which encourage and foster student independence. To promote joyful, spontaneous learning, the guide tells the child he "can" work with the Spindle Boxes rather than he "may" work with the Spindle Boxes. The word "can" affirms the child's new-found abilities whereas "may" implies that the child must seek the guide's permission to perform a task he is ready to undertake. After a student in the Casa receives a presentation, he is at liberty to choose the presented materials any time they are available (i.e. if they are not being used by another student) during his uninterrupted three hour work period. These are two of the tenets of Montessori education that allow spontaneous learning to blossom, freedom of work choice and respect for others.

After a child has received the Spindle Boxes presentation, "The Zero Game" may be introduced. Similar to "Simon Says," The Zero Game is an enjoyable command based activity for young children. The Zero Game also serves as an excellent diversion during transition periods such as when children are waiting in line to use the sink before lunchtime or when waiting for parents to arrive at pick-up time. To play The Zero Game, the guide or assistant invites a group of children to play with her or simply initiates the game with a group in transition. The adult gives a command to a single student that involves a number such as, "Clap your hands eight times, (Name)." The child then performs the action. If younger children who have not yet received any mathematics presentations are playing, the guide limits her commands to "one" or "two" as most children can count that high. An example of a command for a younger child could be, "Jump one time, (Name)."

Once a few numbered commands have been given, the guide introduces a "zero" command such as, "Shout out loud zero times, (Name)." Commands involving "zero" test a child's understanding of the concept of zero as a null or empty category, or in this case, a command to do nothing. These commands are generally reserved for children who have worked independently with the Spindle Boxes. Numbered commands continue as long as time and interest allow.

You can make Spindle Boxes at home. To make Spindle Boxes, purchase one or two compartmentalized boxes (available in stores that carry storage solutions) which contain a total of ten compartments or wooden silverware trays with compartments of equal size with vertical dividers. At home, label the compartments with the numbers "0" through "9." See the illustration "Spindle Boxes in Progress" as an example. Do not include a compartment for "10" as it detracts from one of the purposes of the Spindle Boxes, which is the demonstration that all real numbers can be composed using only the numerals "0" through "9."

Use forty-five ¼" wooden dowels of equal lengths to make spindles. Store these in a basket or wooden box when not in use. Choose colorful ribbon, elastic, or Velcro® strips to make fasteners to tie sets of spindles together. If your child is not yet able to tie a bow, use elastic or Velcro® to facilitate independent use of the Spindle Boxes. Make sure your child always sits when using Spindle Boxes for safety. Following gameplay, store all materials in a safe place away from younger children to prevent falls on objects and the possibility of poking eyes.

Once your child has worked with the Spindle Boxes, you can play The Zero Game with your child. Give numbered commands such as "Hop three times," interspersed with "zero commands" such as, "Tap your foot zero times." Play as long as time and interest allow.

Cards and Counters

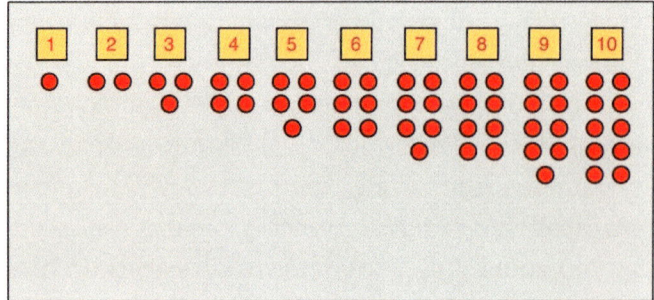

Following individual work with Spindle Boxes, the guide introduces "Cards and Counters" for additional counting practice. While there is no official time frame for the introduction of Cards and Counters, the general guideline is to present the first lesson when the child becomes bored with Spindle Boxes. Cards and Counters activities reinforce the following concepts:

- Each number is a separate quantity.
- The sequence of numerals from 1 through 10 is verifiable.
- Correspondence between quantity and written numbers is shown.
- Odd and even numbers are illustrated by the arrangement of the counters. Even numbers are in pairs; odd numbers have a counter that is offset from the pairs.
- Counters arranged in pairs visually prepare children for division by two.

Cards and Counters consists of a set of wooden number cards labeled "1" through "10" and fifty-five identical counters, usually red wooden disks. To begin the Cards and Counters presentation, the guide places the Cards and Counters materials on a rug or on a long table. Under the guide's direction, the child removes the number cards from their box and places them at the bottom of the work surface at random. The guide places the "1" number card on the far upper left-hand side of the rug and asks the child what comes next. When the child finds the number card for "2," the guide has him place it next to the "1" number card. She gives the point of interest that the child should leave three fingers-width of space between each card. If necessary, the guide demonstrates how much space to leave between the cards. Once the child understands how to leave space, he lays out the remaining number cards in order from left to right.

As soon as the number cards are laid out across the top of the rug as in the illustration "Cards and Counters," the guide counts one red disk counter aloud and places it under the number card for "1," careful to leave some space between the bottom of the card and the counter. To count "2," she places one disk below and to the left of the "2" card. As she places the counter, she says "one." She places the second counter to its right, leaving some space between the two counters, and counts, "two." To count "3," she places the first two counters one at a time as with the "2" number card and counts aloud. The third counter is placed below the two counters in the middle, as illustrated in this book. To count "4," the guide counts aloud one number at a time as she places the counters in pairs. This formation gives a concrete representation of the two times tables in multiplication and division by two in preparation for future mathematics studies. Now that the pattern for placing counters is established, the child labels the remaining number cards with the correct number of counters. The guide supervises with a minimum of commentary. When all counters are placed, the guide mentions how there are no counters left in the original container. This control of error helps the child realize that if he does the work correctly, all counters should be used.

Following independent work with Cards and Counters, the guide introduces the related activity, "Odd and Even Numbers." Depending on the child's level of interest and confidence, Odd and Even Numbers can be introduced immediately following the Cards and Counters presentation. If the child becomes absorbed in Cards and Counters work, the guide may wait for a more opportune time to introduce Odd and Even Numbers. Since the child has already had experience counting sets of quantities with Spindle Box materials, typically there should not be a long delay between the Cards and Counters lesson and the Odd and Even Numbers presentation.

To introduce Odd and Even Numbers, the guide has the child lay out all the cards and counters as in the illustration "Cards and Counters." Once the materials are arranged, the guide points out how some number cards have counters that are arranged with a disk in the middle and some do not. She says, "The numbers with a counter in the middle are odd numbers. The numbers without a counter in the middle are even numbers." To concretely emphasize this distinction, the guide places her index finger under the number card "1" and slides her finger vertically until it reaches the single counter. When her finger hits the disk, she says, "Stop." Without further commentary, the guide lifts her finger and places it under the "2" number card. She slides her finger between the two counters, continuing until she reaches the bottom of the rug. The guide may make a "whoosh" sound as she slides her fingers between the counters to emphasize how there are no counters in the middle to stop her, similar to how a car can "whoosh" by without stopping when on an open road with no obstacles. If necessary, the guide tells the child, "My finger could keep going forever and ever. There are no counters in the way to stop it." The guide demonstrates this action with all remaining numbers, always saying "stop" with odd numbers and "whoosh" or remaining silent with even numbers.

After kinesthetically demonstrating the difference between odd and even numbers, the guide slides the odd numbered cards to the top of the rug. She points to each odd numbered card in turn and says, "These numbers are 'odd.'" The guide then points to each even numbered card in turn and says, "These numbers are 'even.'" To solidify the child's memory of the terms "odd" and "even," the guide launches into a Three Period Lesson, a game-like technique used to introduce and review vocabulary in the Casa.

The first period of the Three Period Lesson is called "Naming." The guide already named the vocabulary when she pointed to the top row of cards and said, "These numbers are 'odd.'" When pointing to the second row of number cards, she said, "These numbers are 'even.'" This concludes the first period of the Three Period Lesson for "odd" and "even."

The second period of the Three Period Lesson is called "Recognition." This is the game-like portion of the Three Period Lesson. During this stage, the guide gives commands involving odd and even number cards such as, "Hand me an odd number," "Point to another odd number," or "Pick up an even number." The guide continues to give commands until the child is accurate and confident, or loses interest.

The third period of the Three Period Lesson is called "Remembering." To test the child's memory of odd and even numbers, the guide points to a number card at random and asks, "What kind of number is this?" If this question is too vague for the child, the guide can modify her question by asking, "Is this an odd number or an even number?" After the child says whether the number is odd or even, the guide points to another card at random and asks the same question. If at any time the child gives the incorrect answer, the guide simply states the correct answer without criticism. The guide can always review odd and even numbers at a later time if necessary.

To review odd and even numbers, the guide may play the "Bring Me Game" with an individual student or small group of children. During the Bring Me Game for Odd and Even Numbers, all number cards from Cards and Counters are laid out at random on a rug or table. Counters are not used in this activity. The guide sits at a distant rug or table and gives a "Bring Me" command to one of the children playing such as, "Bring me a number that is odd." The child to whom the command was directed retrieves any odd number card from the first table or rug and shows it to the guide. If the child is correct, the guide says, "You brought me an odd number. You can take the odd number back." Once the child returns, the guide gives additional commands. If the guide is playing with one child, she continues to give commands until every number card has been retrieved at least once, or until the student loses interest. When playing with a small group of children, the guide gives commands to one child at a time. In a group setting, the game continues until each child has had at least one turn.

You can make your own Cards and Counters set at home to reinforce your child's mathematical studies. Make ten cards, each one labeled with a number from 1 to 10, and use fifty-five identical small objects, such as buttons, as counters. Store all cards and counters in a secure place following use as counters can be a choking hazard. Keep all Cards and Counters materials away from younger children for safety.

Memory Game of Numbers

Following mastery of all Number Rods, Sandpaper Numerals, Spindle Boxes, and Cards and Counters activities, the "Memory Game of Numbers" is introduced as a fun mathematics assessment tool. In the Casa, no standardized tests are administered in order to determine a child's understanding and mastery of mathematical concepts. Instead, a game that covers all previously learned Mathematics manipulatives is presented to celebrate the child's knowledge and show the guide which areas need improvement. The Memory Game of Numbers is the first of these mathematic assessment activities in the Casa. The Memory Game of Numbers serves the following purposes:

- The child's short term memory of numerical symbols and their corresponding quantities is practiced and developed.
- The concept of "0" is both concretely and abstractly reinforced.
- Through the Memory Game of Numbers, the student learns to transfer his knowledge of the numbers 0-10 to concrete objects in the environment.

The Memory Game of Numbers is a group game which requires two to eleven players. For a group of eleven players, each child in the game draws one folded slip of paper from a dish. Each slip of paper contains one numerical symbol between "0" and "10" inclusively. To keep the number inside each slip hidden from view, paper slips are often placed in tiny bags sewn by the guide.

Once each child has drawn a paper slip, he takes it out of the bag, peeks at the number inside, and then sets it aside out of view from the other players. It is helpful if the child tucks the paper slip back into the bag or under the rug where everyone is gathered. Whenever possible, the guide chooses the oldest, most experienced child in the group to take the first turn so he can serve as a model to the other less experienced players. When everyone has had a chance to look at his number slip, the guide chooses a child and says, "Bring me your number of something in the room, (Name)." If these directions are too vague, the guide may instead request that the child retrieve his number of specific objects as in, "Bring me your number of buttons." If the child's number slip says "8," he should find eight buttons, place them on a tray, and bring the tray to the rug. The guide will then ask the student what he brought. He should reply that he brought eight buttons. The guide may also ask to see his number slip. It is not required that the child count the objects aloud in front of the group as counting has typically already been mastered at this point.

After the first child retrieves the number of objects specified on his card, the guide has him put the items back where he found them before another child takes a turn. While waiting for the child to return, the guide may take the opportunity to casually chat with the waiting students about counting and numbers. She may also mention what the student who is putting the items away is doing. For instance, the guide may say something like, "Look at where (Name) is going with all those buttons! How many buttons did he bring to the rug again?... That's right! He brought eight buttons. I wonder where he got the buttons from? Oh, it looks like (Name) is putting the buttons back in the box from the Sewing a Button activity." By speaking to the children who are waiting, the guide helps ward off impatience while simultaneously reinforcing language development, number facts, and organization of the room.

Once the child returns, the guide chooses another child to retrieve his number of objects. When playing with eleven children, the game continues until everyone has had a turn. If fewer than eleven children are playing, each child takes a number slip, memorizes it, and retrieves objects as directed. As soon as each child in the group of fewer than eleven has had at least one turn, the used number slips are set aside and students draw a new slip to begin another round. The game continues until all the number slips are accounted for or at least until "0" has been drawn.

Regardless of the size of the group playing the Memory Game of Numbers, one of the most important aspects of the activity is when a child draws the number "0." When a child is called upon to retrieve his number of objects, and his number is "0," his actions show the guide whether or not he understands the concept of zero as an empty set. Often times, a child who has drawn "0" will return with an empty tray or an empty vase. Regardless of what the child brings to illustrate the concept of zero, the guide may elicit a verbal definition from the student by saying something like, "Oh! You haven't brought anything. Did you need to look at your number again?" A child usually replies that his number was zero, so he brought nothing at all! The guide may rejoice in her student understanding the concept of "0" by saying, "That's right. '0' means 'nothing.'" She is very careful to not upset sensitive children who would not respond well to her commentary about how he had not brought anything to the rug. Instead of making an issue of the empty set, the guide may simply ask the child, "What did you bring?" The guide knows how to handle the "0" with each child based upon her observations over an extended period of time. Keep in mind that individual students react differently upon drawing "0." Some children find it amusing to draw "0" while others find it disappointing. Either way, most children adjust to the mechanics of the game over time.[2]   Repetition of the game increases the chance that a child will eventually draw every number from 0 through 10 at least once during his stay in the Casa. This element of chance may encourage children to continue playing the Memory Game of Numbers throughout the year, thereby strengthening their short and long term memories of numerical symbols and their equivalent quantities.

Although the Memory Game of Numbers acts as an assessment tool for the guide to determine a child's level of mastery of the numbers zero through ten, younger children can play alongside their older peers if interested. If a young child wants to join the Memory Game of Numbers but does not know how to count, he chooses an older child in the Casa to help him retrieve the correct number of objects. This is one of the many advantages of having a mixed-age group of three through six year olds in a Primary Montessori Casa. When a younger child participates in the Memory Game of Numbers alongside older peers, he becomes immersed in the world of mathematics in preparation for future studies. His older peers also benefit from this practice. By assisting a younger child in the Memory Game of Numbers, older children in the Casa naturally practice the virtues of patience and kindness. Helping a younger child is also an excellent confidence booster to support strong self-esteem. Finally, by helping younger peers, older children gain additional practice with the materials presented as they must slow down and think about the work carefully.

You can play the Memory Game of Numbers at home with your child, his siblings, and other family members. Create eleven identical number cards from cardstock. Write one number per card from 0 to 10 on the back of each card with indelible ink. Place number cards in a bag or dish so players can choose a card at random. Montessori teachers often place each number card in a separate hand-sewn cotton bag for secrecy and aesthetics. Each small bag is then placed

[2] Montessori, Maria. *The Discovery of the Child.* Trans. Mary A. Johnstone. Chennai: Kalakshetra, 2006. Print. Pages 303-306.

in a larger bag, on a dish, or in a basket.

Once you have created your Memory Game of Numbers set, you can begin the game. Each player draws one card and discreetly peeks at his number. Players take turns retrieving their number of articles in the room. Depending on your child's confidence, you can give him a specific task such as, "Bring your number of pencils to the rug," or use a general command such as, "Bring your number of something in the room to the rug." When your child returns, you can ask him how many items he brought to the rug. Check his number card to confirm accuracy. If your child has retrieved the incorrect number of articles, say what he has brought and ask him to bring you the number of items on his card. For instance, you may say, "Oh, you brought me '6.' Now bring me what your card says. What does your card say?" Usually this is enough for a child to correct his error. If your child constantly retrieves the incorrect number of items, it may mean he needs additional work with foundational exercises that strengthen understanding of the quantities and numbers zero through ten. Preliminary activities for quantity and number correspondence review include Number Rods and Cards, Spindle Boxes, and Cards and Counters. Your child may also require additional practice with earlier activities to improve his short and long term memory of numbers, particularly distance games such as Choose a Card, Find the Rod and Choose a Rod, Find the Card with the Number Rods and Cards. Consult *My First Montessori Book of Quantities* for more information and additional suggestions. If your child becomes frustrated, gently end the game by saying, "Thank you for playing with me. We can look at this some other time."

If your child has retrieved the correct number of articles, he returns the items to their proper place. When he returns, the next player takes his turn. If you have fewer than eleven players, set the used number cards aside and draw again. Continue playing until someone draws the number 0 or until all numbers have been drawn.

Mastery of the Memory Game of Numbers indicates readiness for future mathematics work. After learning the numbers zero through ten, students in the Casa begin to explore the decimal system and work with numbers into the thousands. Eventually, equations in the four operations of mathematics (addition, subtraction, multiplication, and division) are applied to numbers into the millions and fractions. To explore quantities and numbers beyond "10" with your child, consider reading *My First Montessori Book of Teen Numbers* as the next step in building a solid mathematics foundation for elementary school.

Other Mathematics Titles
in the
My First Montessori Book Series

My First Montessori Book of Quantities

My First Montessori Book of Teen Numbers

My First Montessori Book of Tens

My First Montessori Book of Bead Counting to 100

My First Montessori Book of Skip Counting

My First Montessori Book of Square Numbers

My First Montessori Book of Fractions

For a complete list of titles, visit the author's website at:

http://themontessorimysteryunveiled.weebly.com

13201332R00031

Printed in Great Britain
by Amazon.co.uk, Ltd.,
Marston Gate.